Love in Peaces Coloring Book

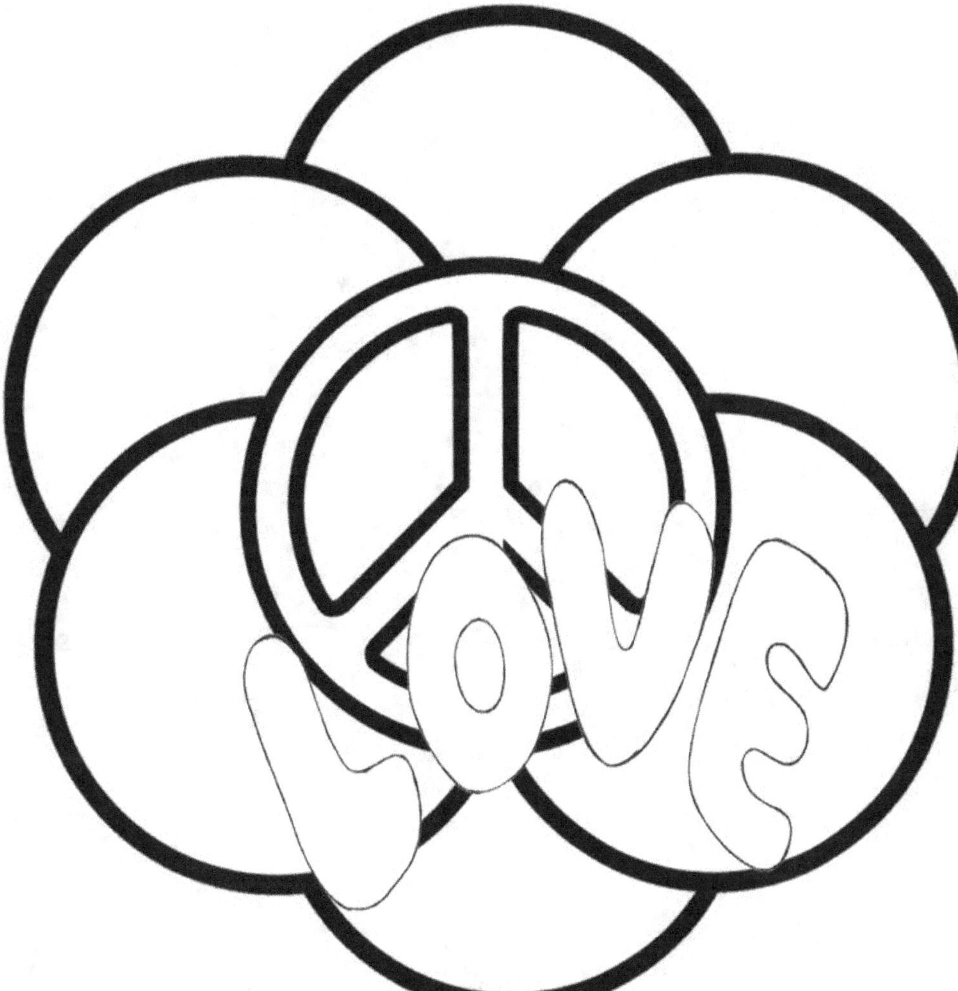

Nina Packer

Love in Peaces Coloring Book

Copyright: Published in the United States by Nina Packer
Published January 2018

ISBN-13: 978-1983929892

ISBN-10: 1983929891

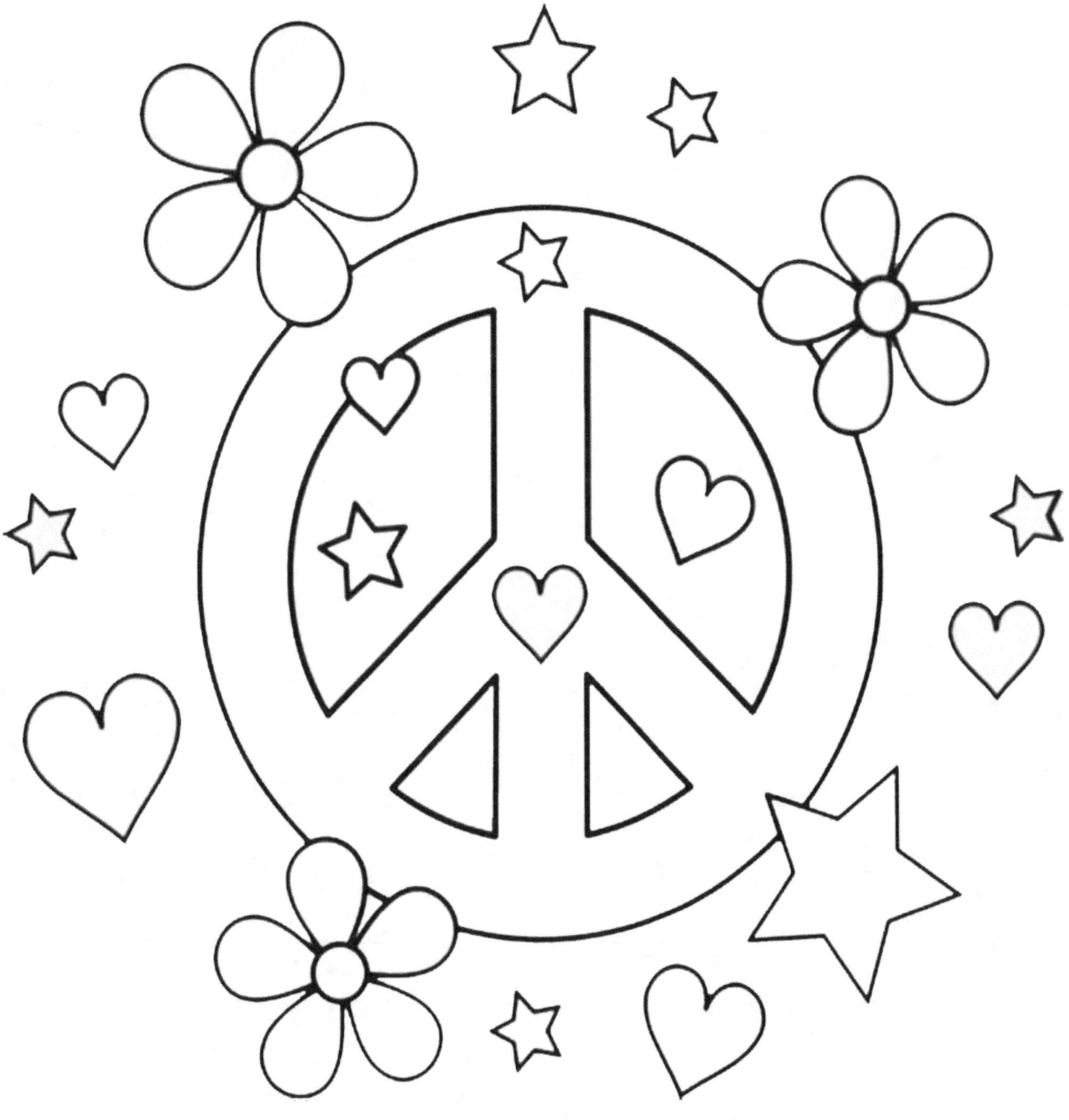

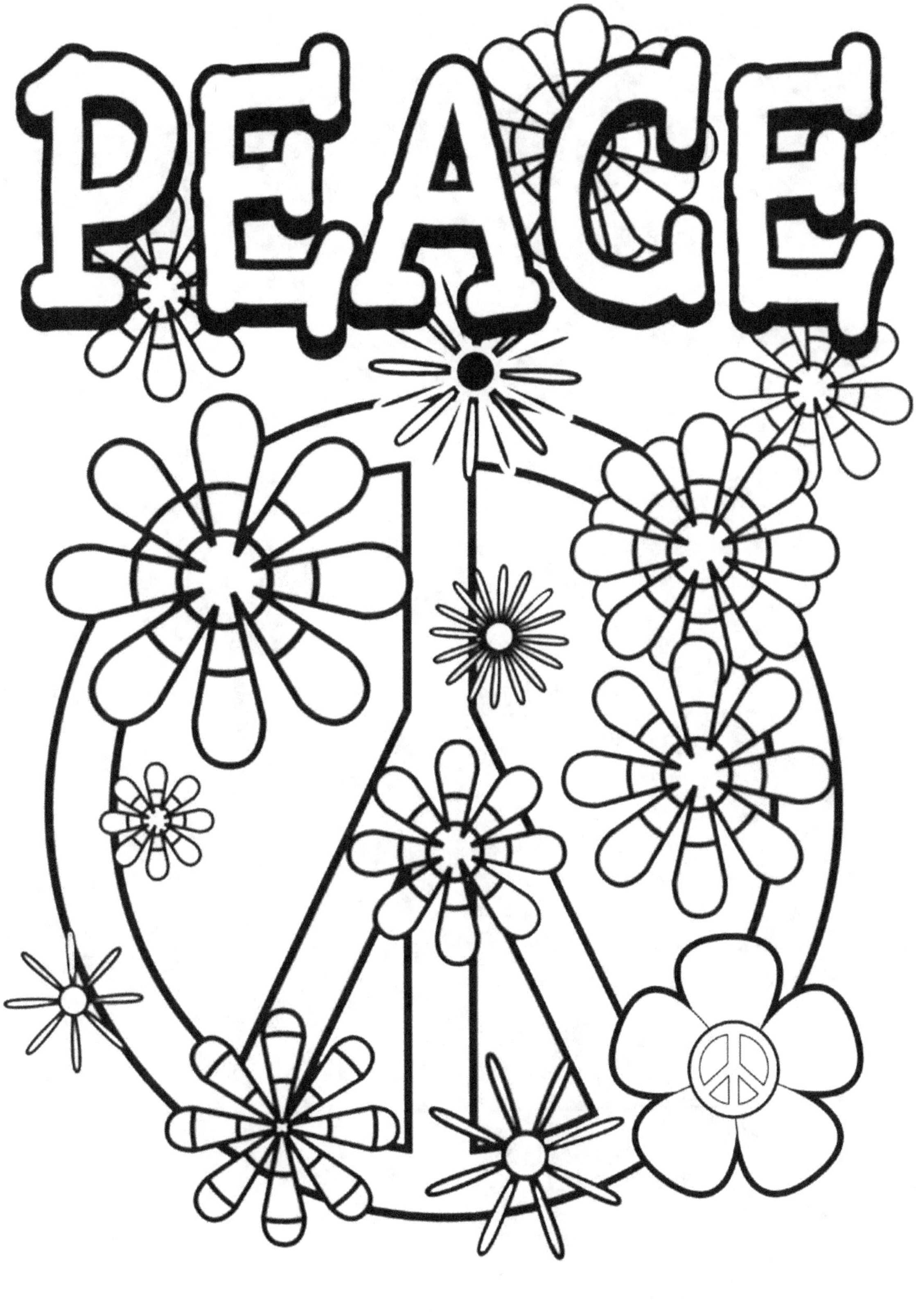
PEACE

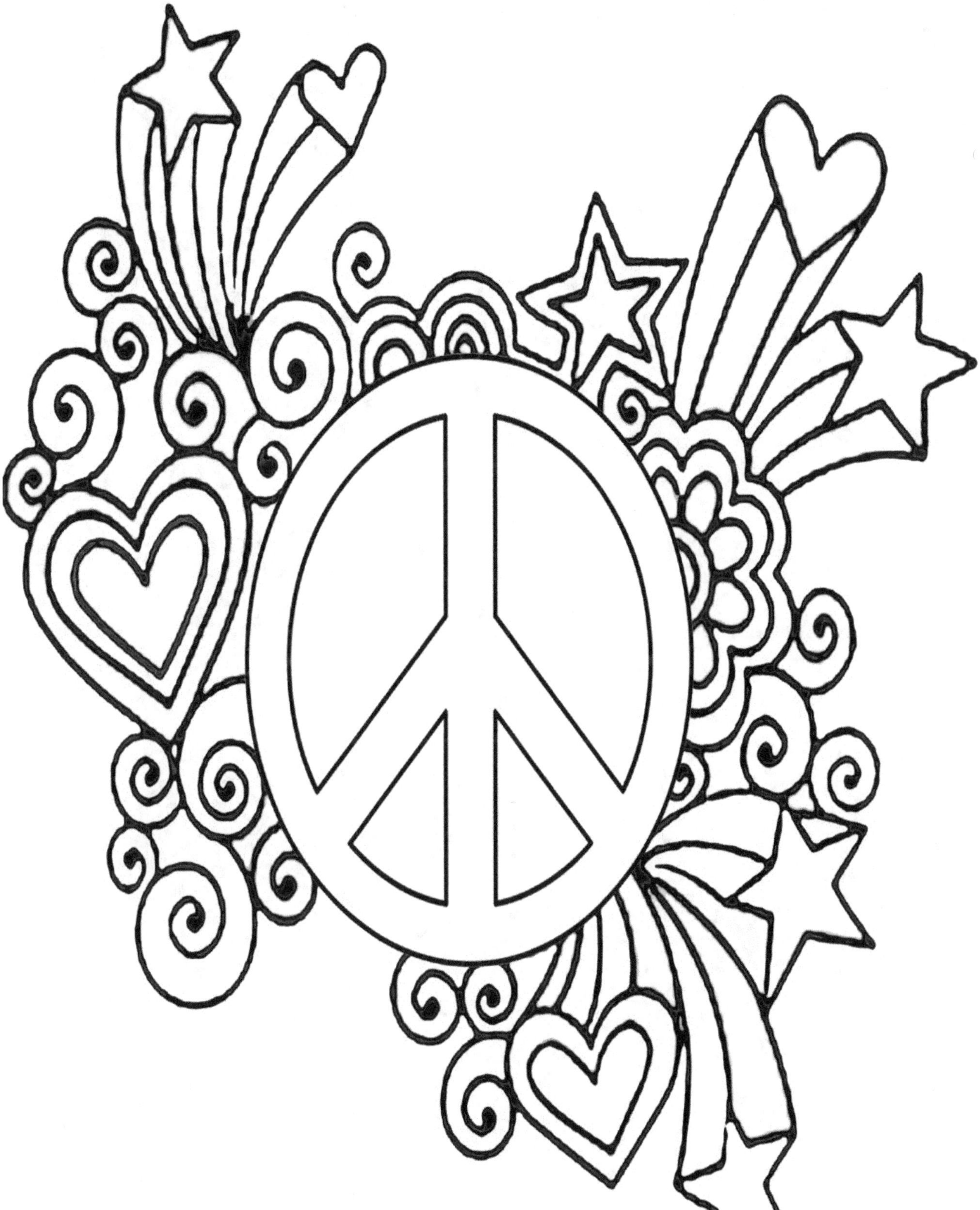

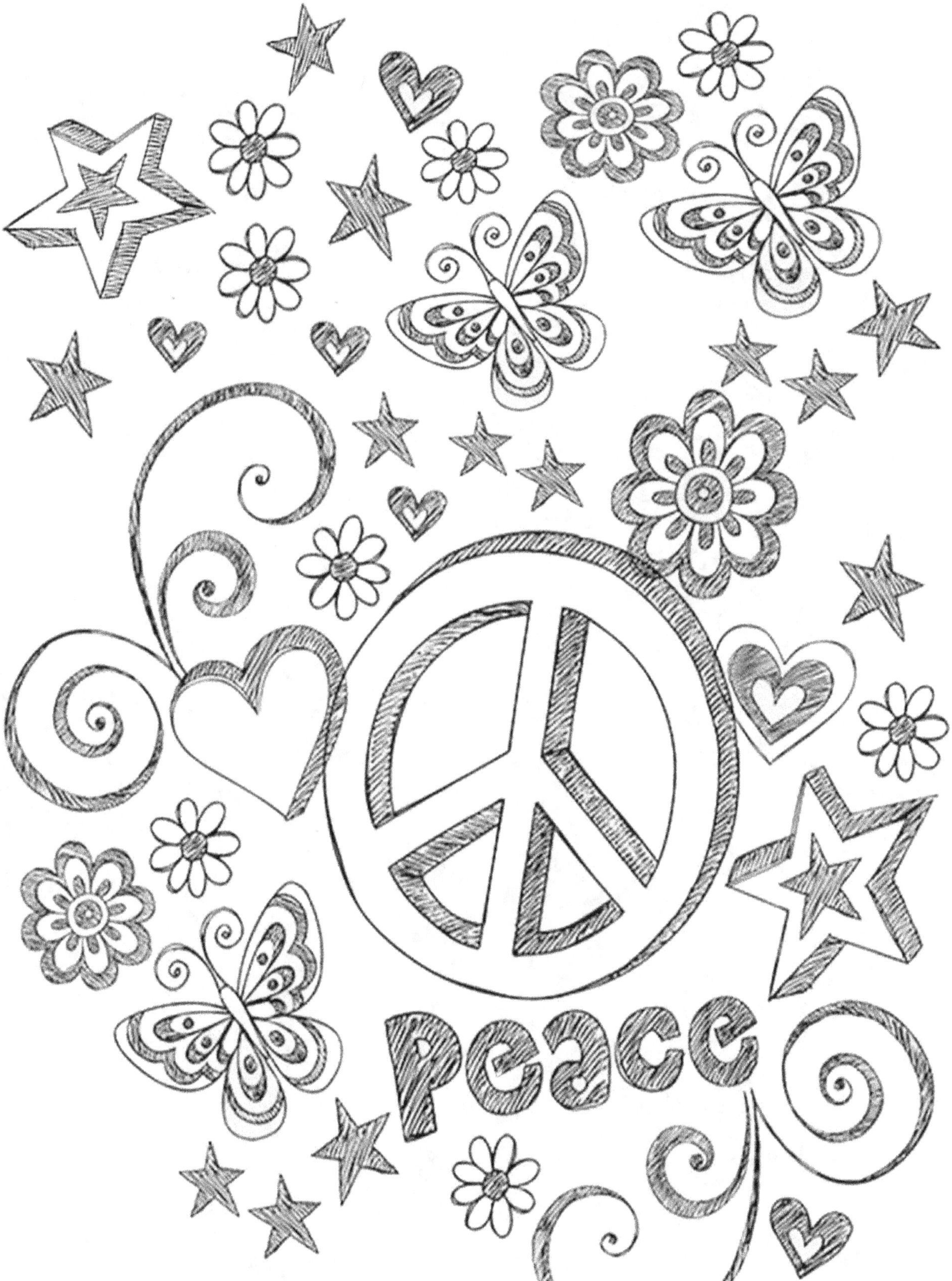
peace

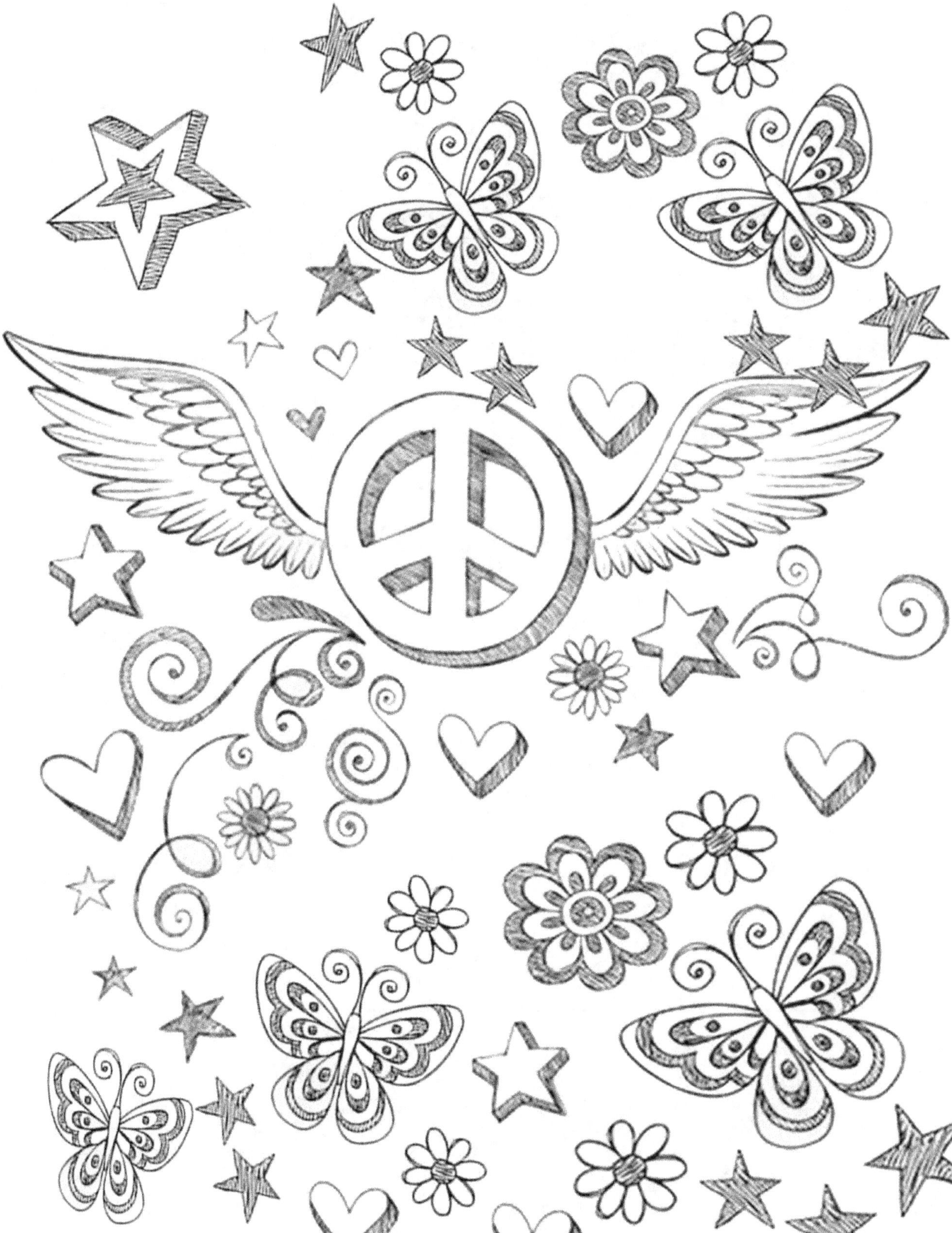

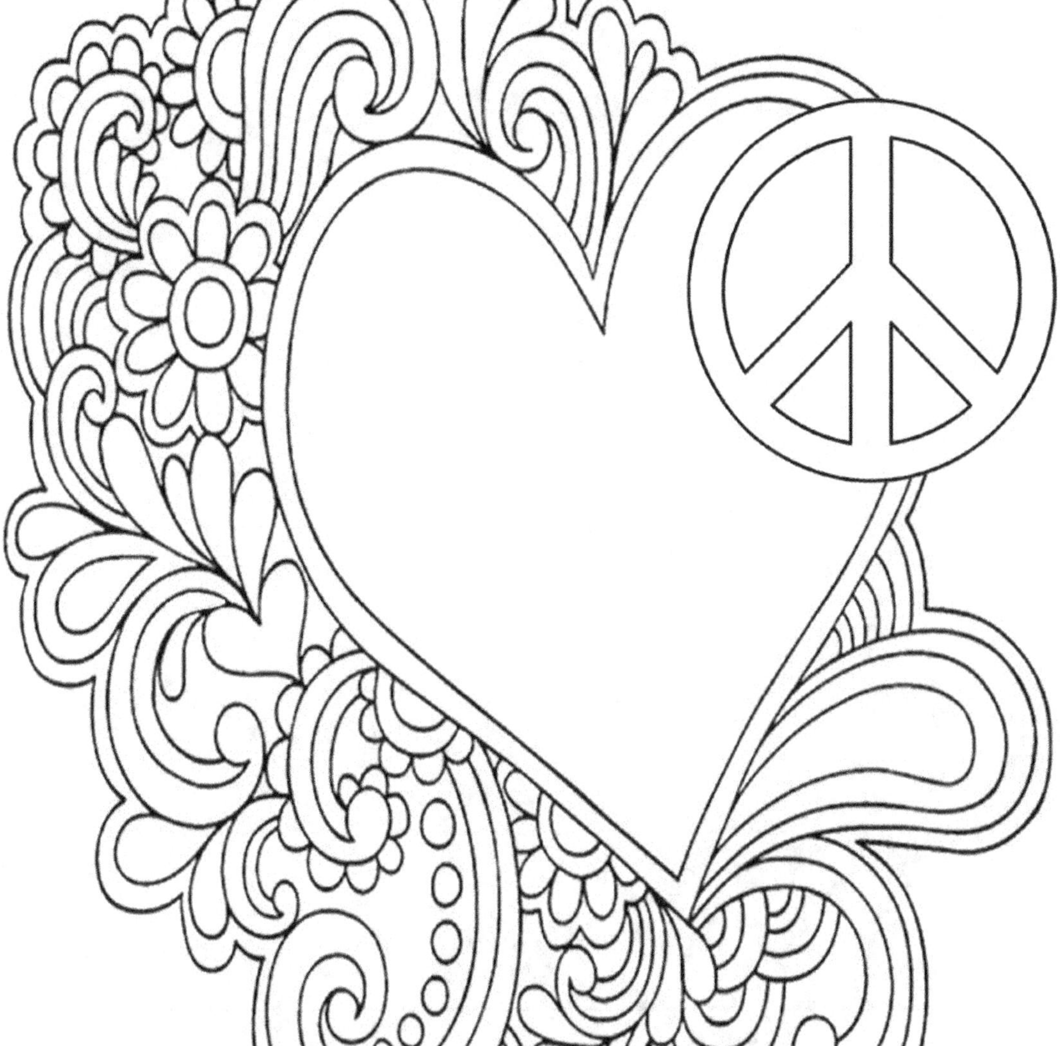

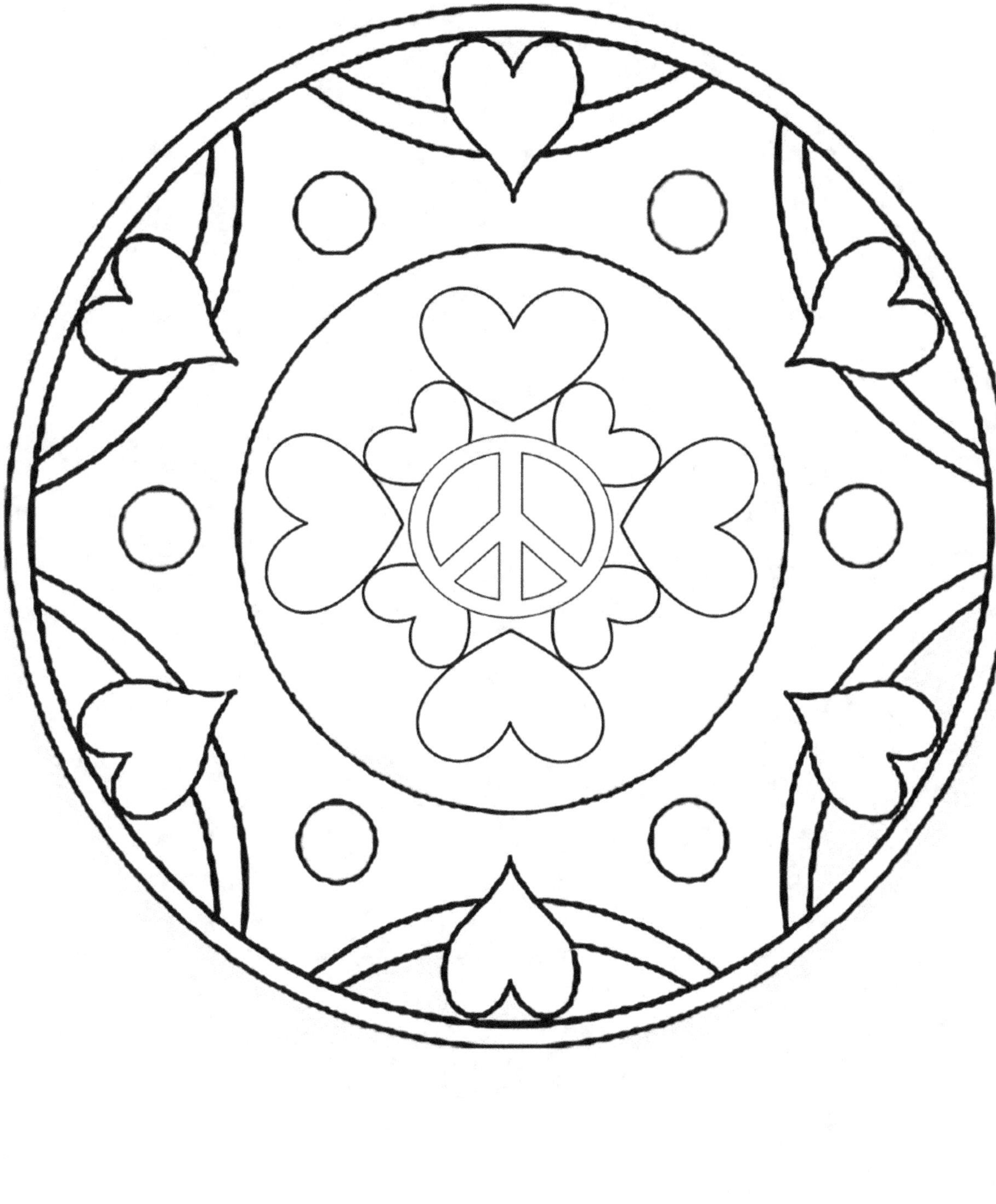

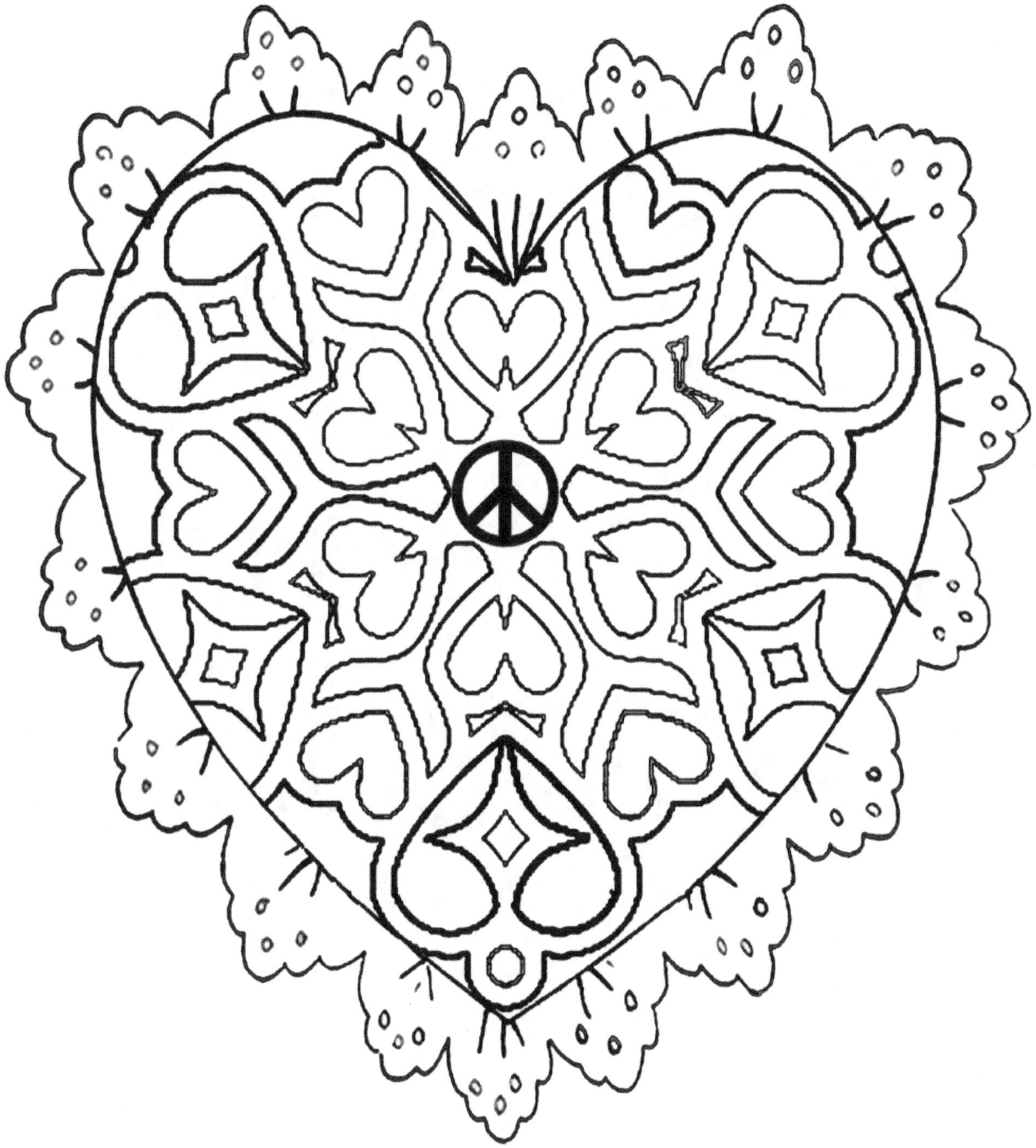

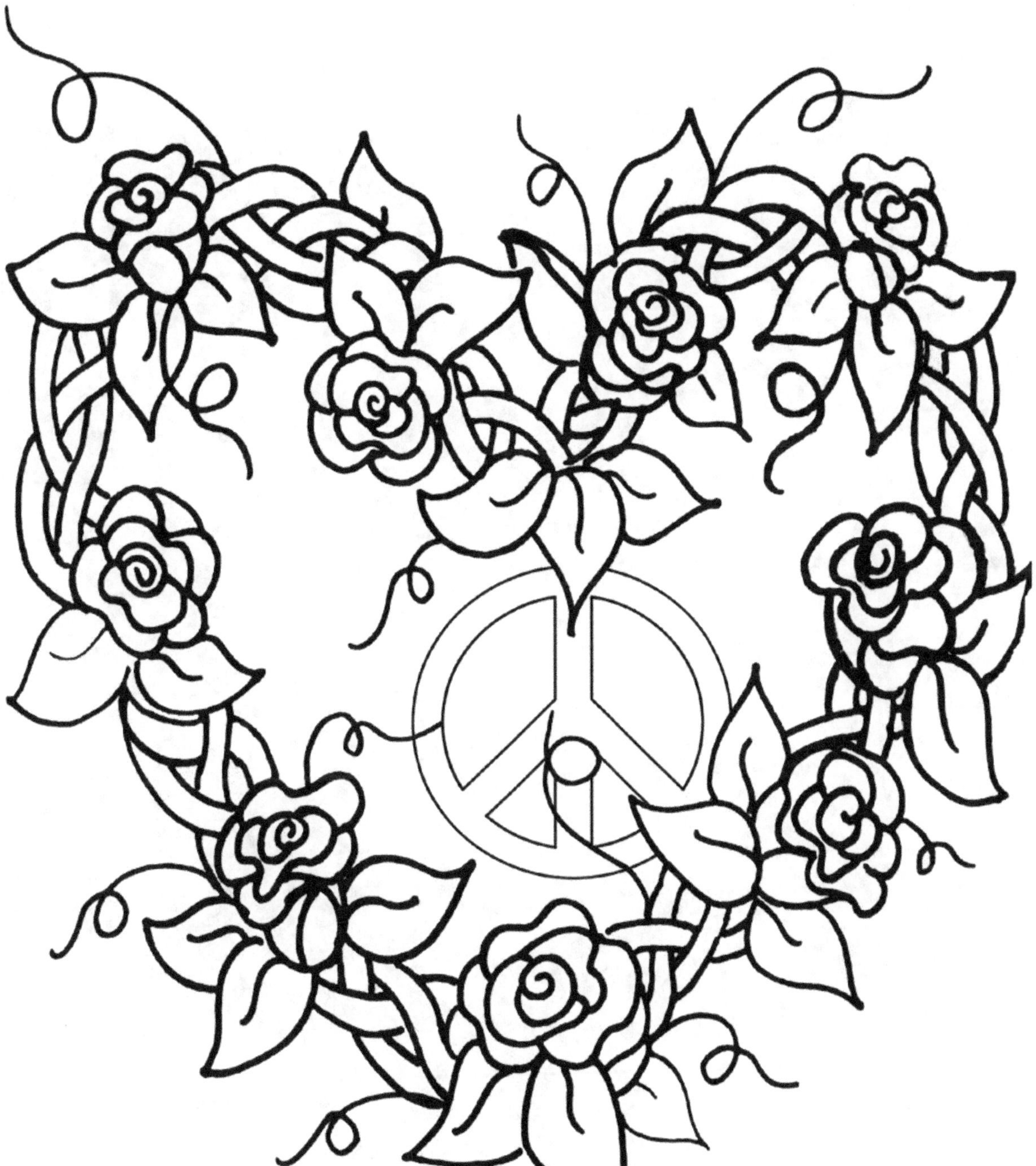

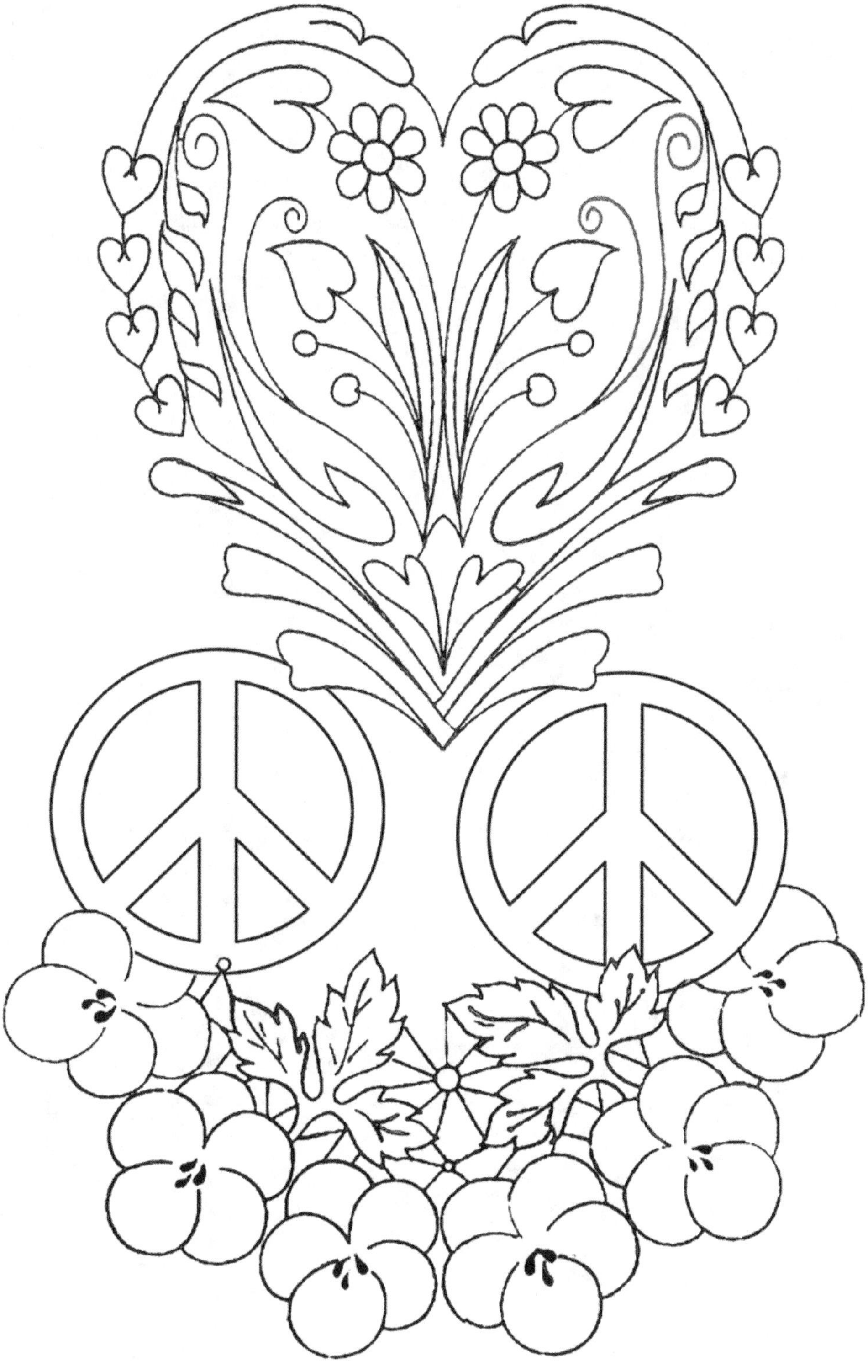

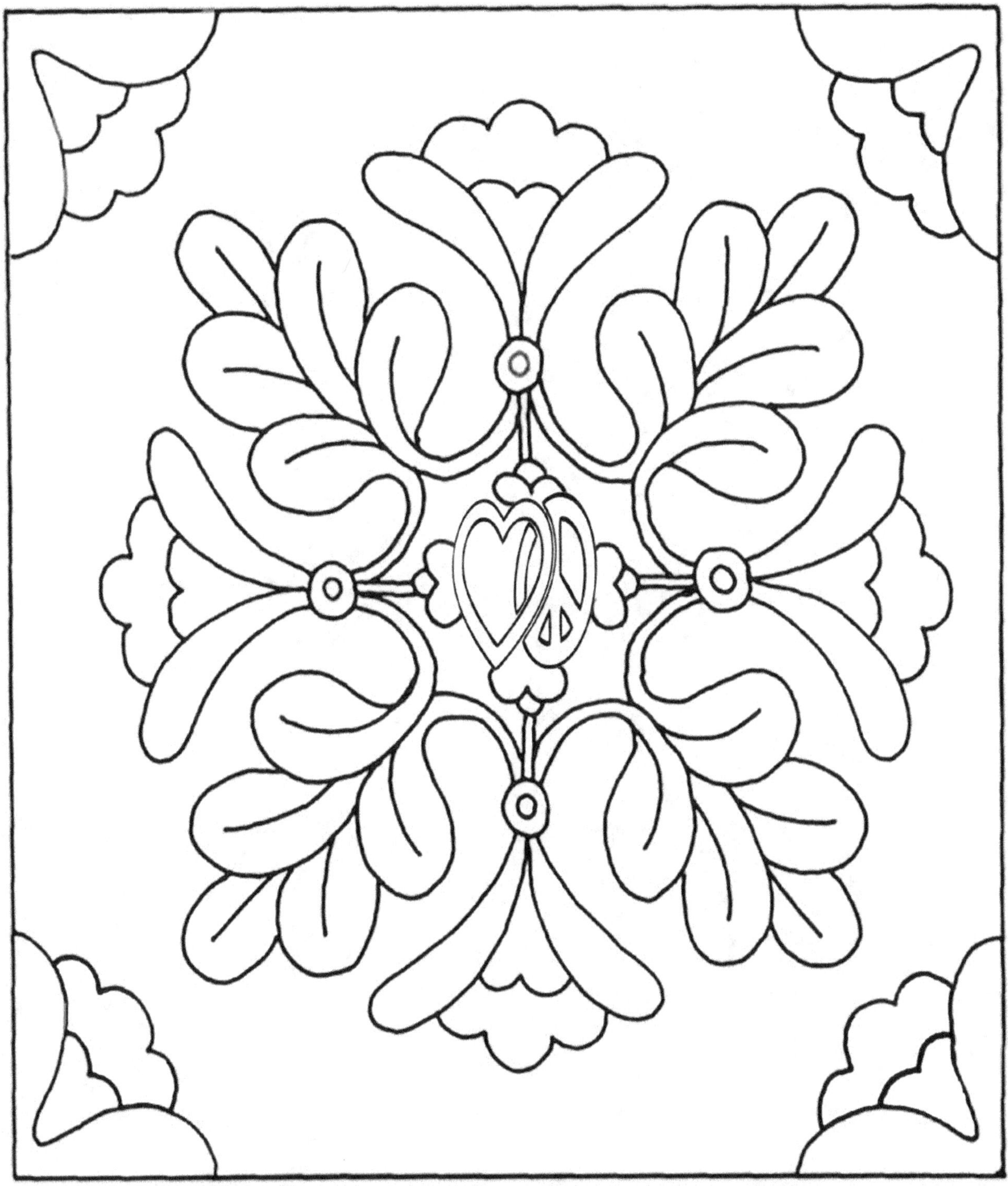

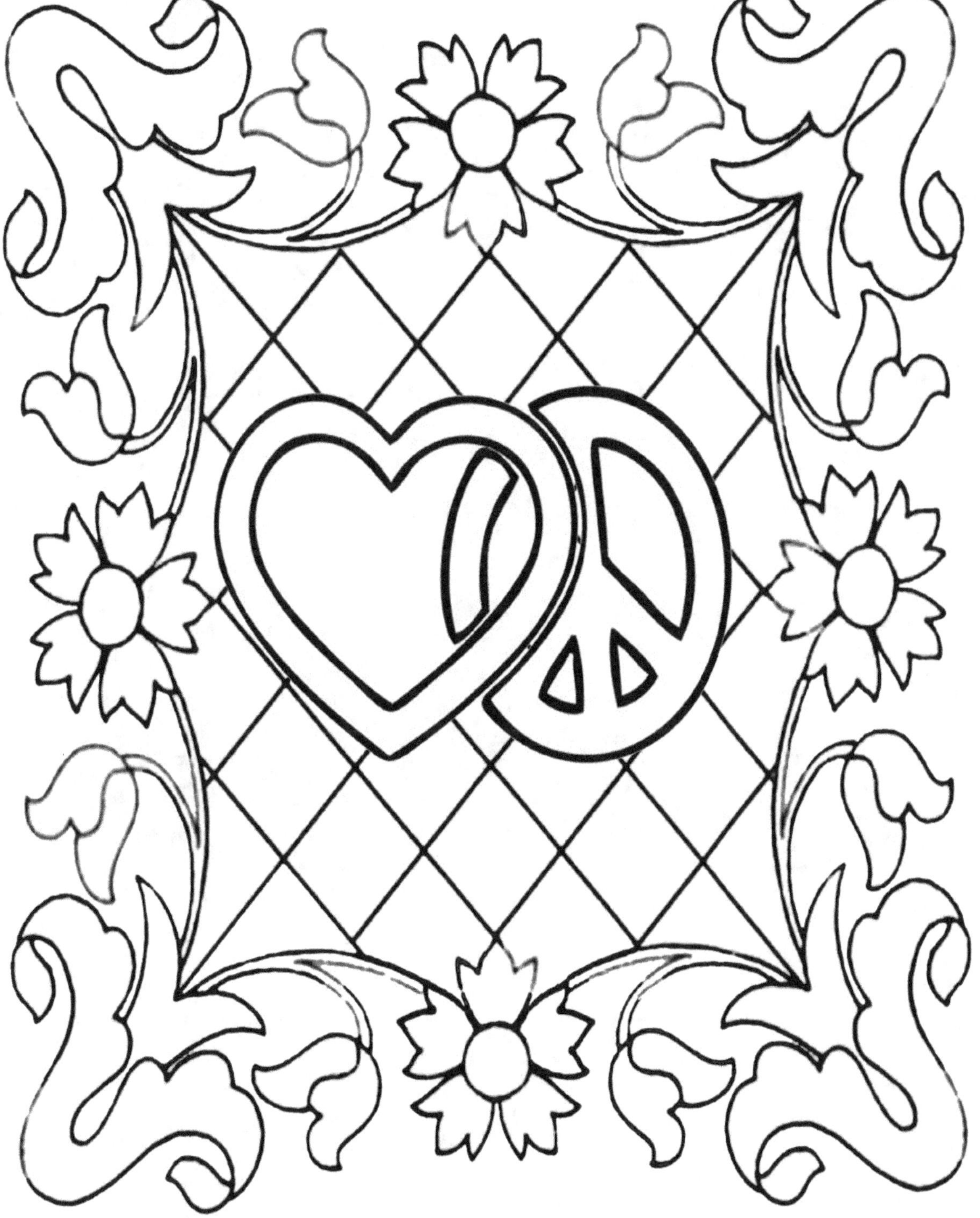

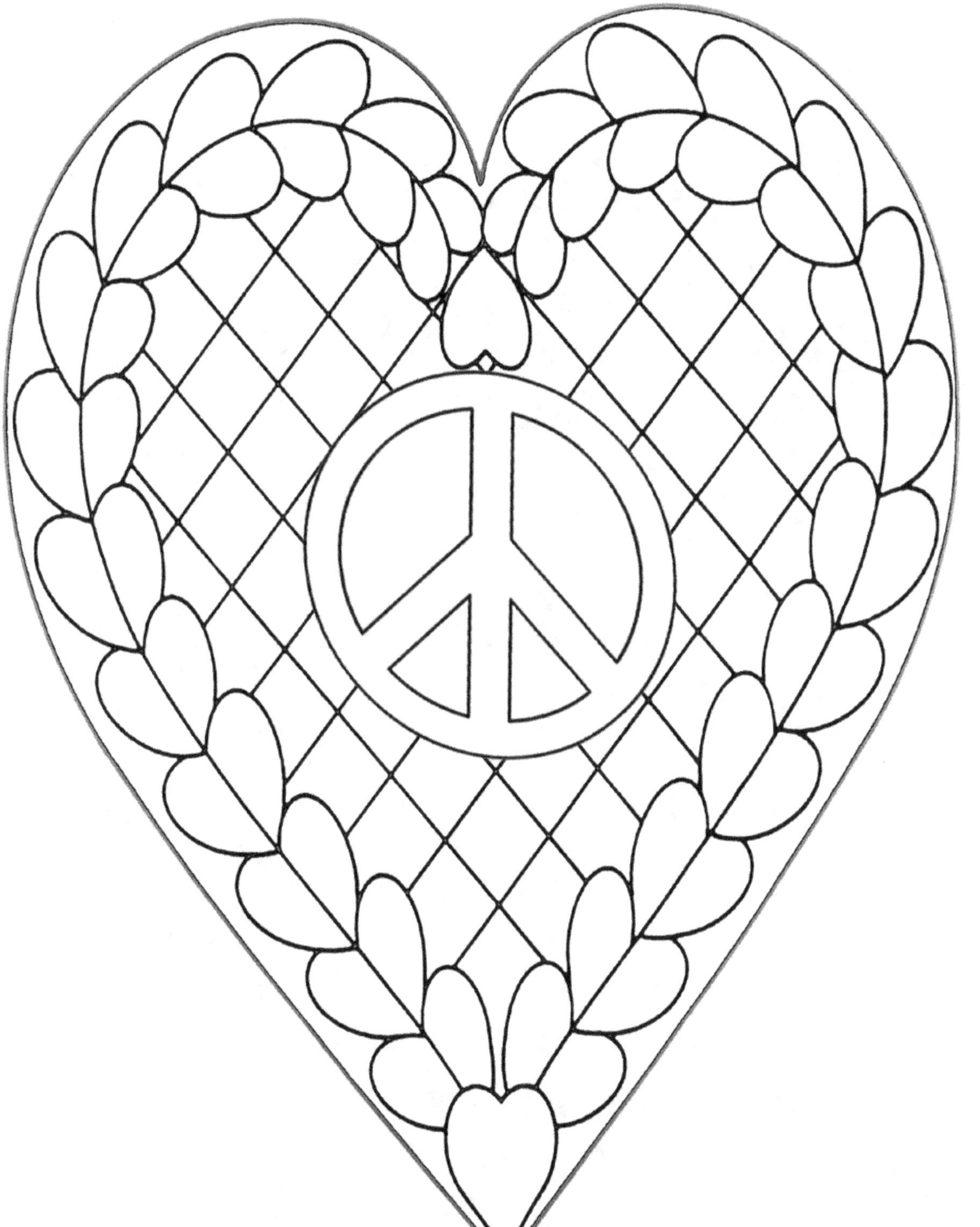

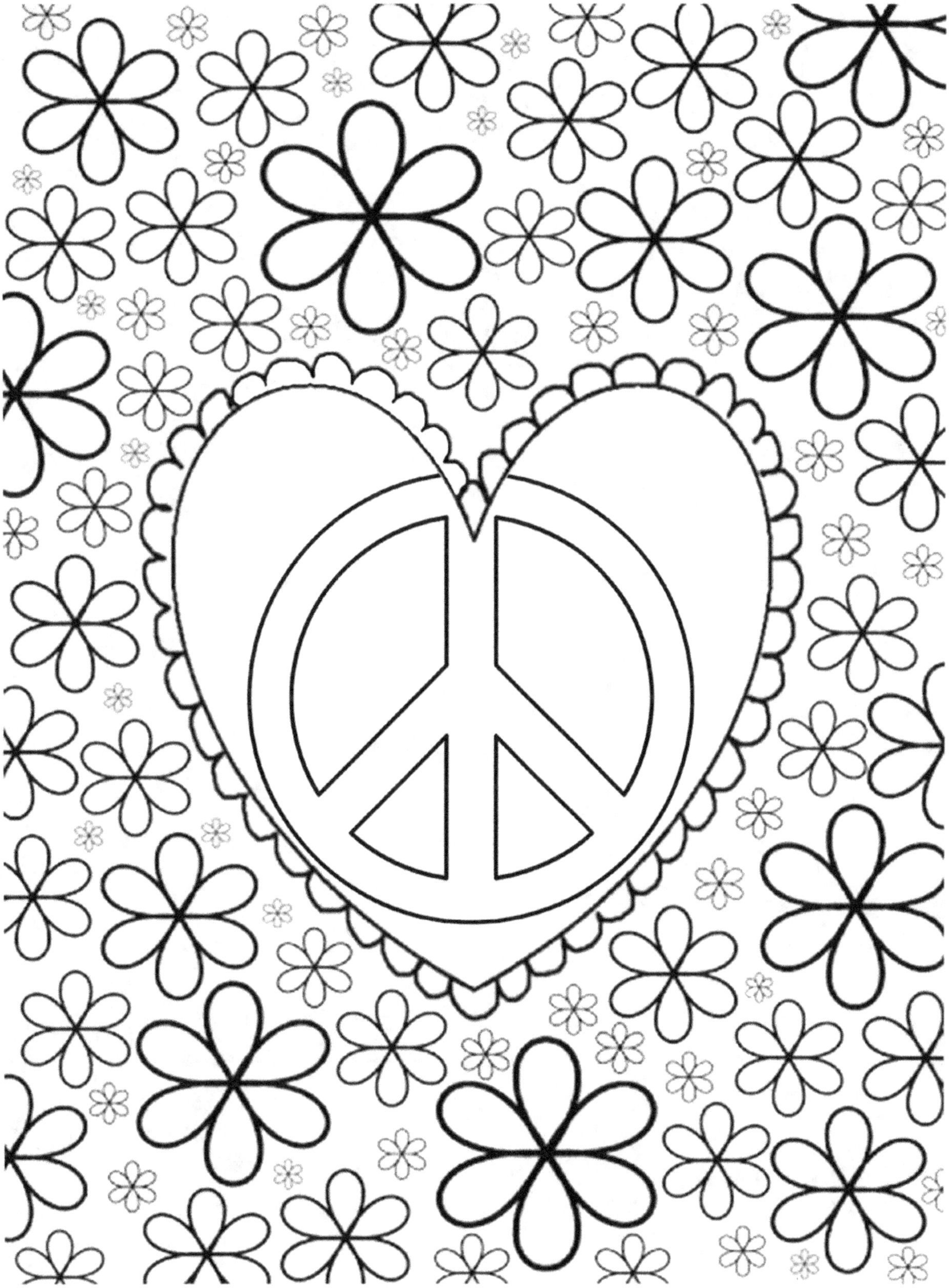

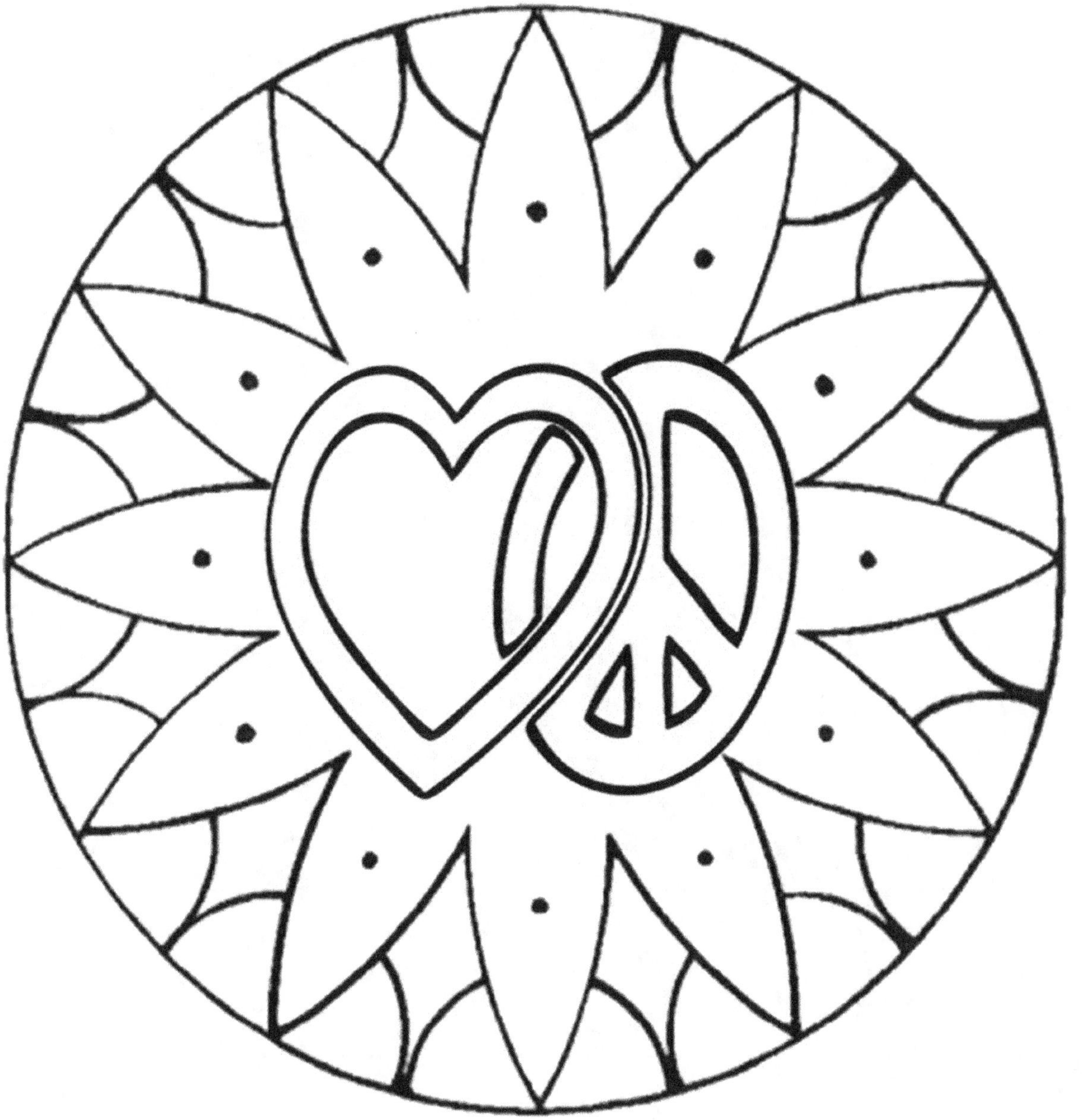

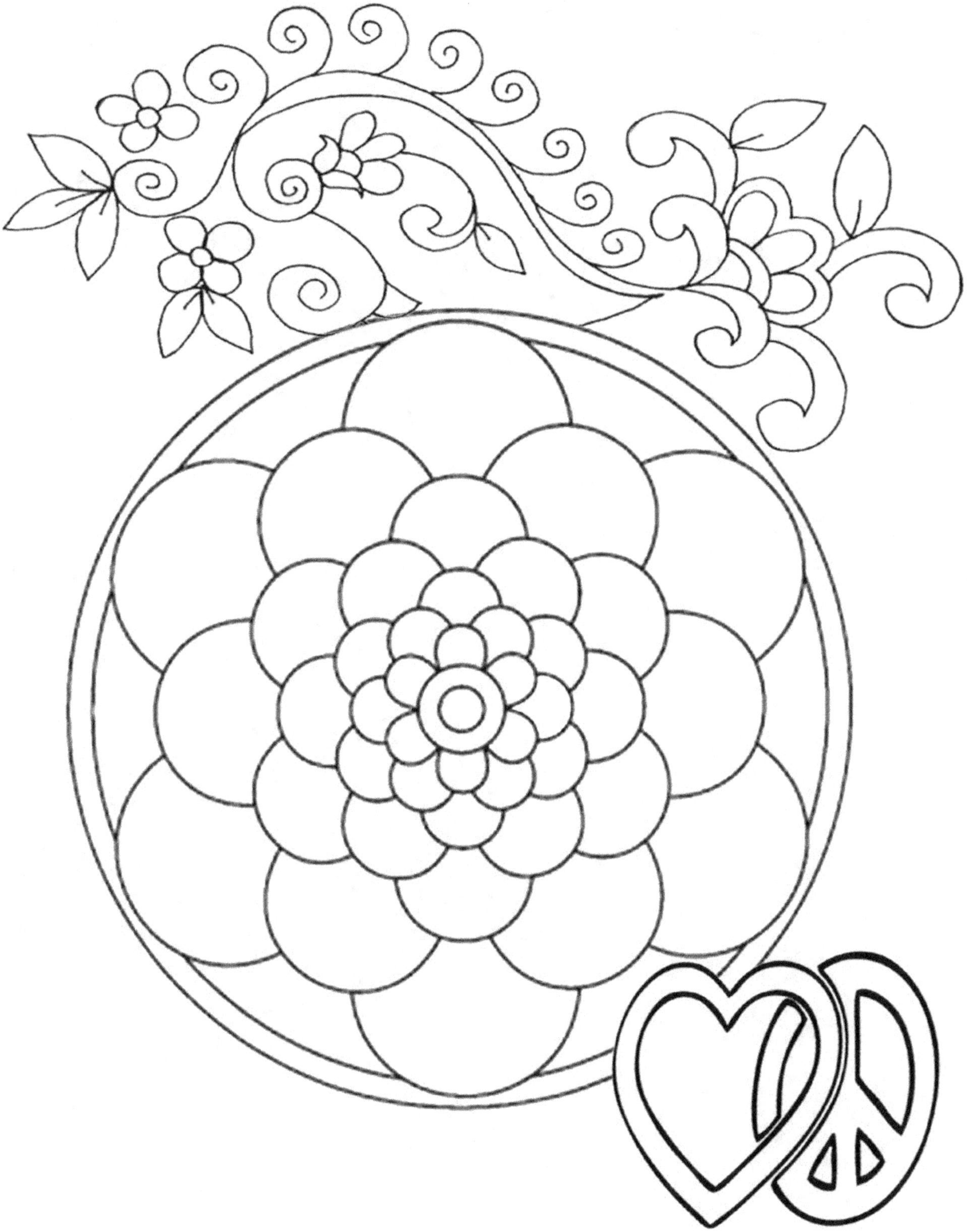

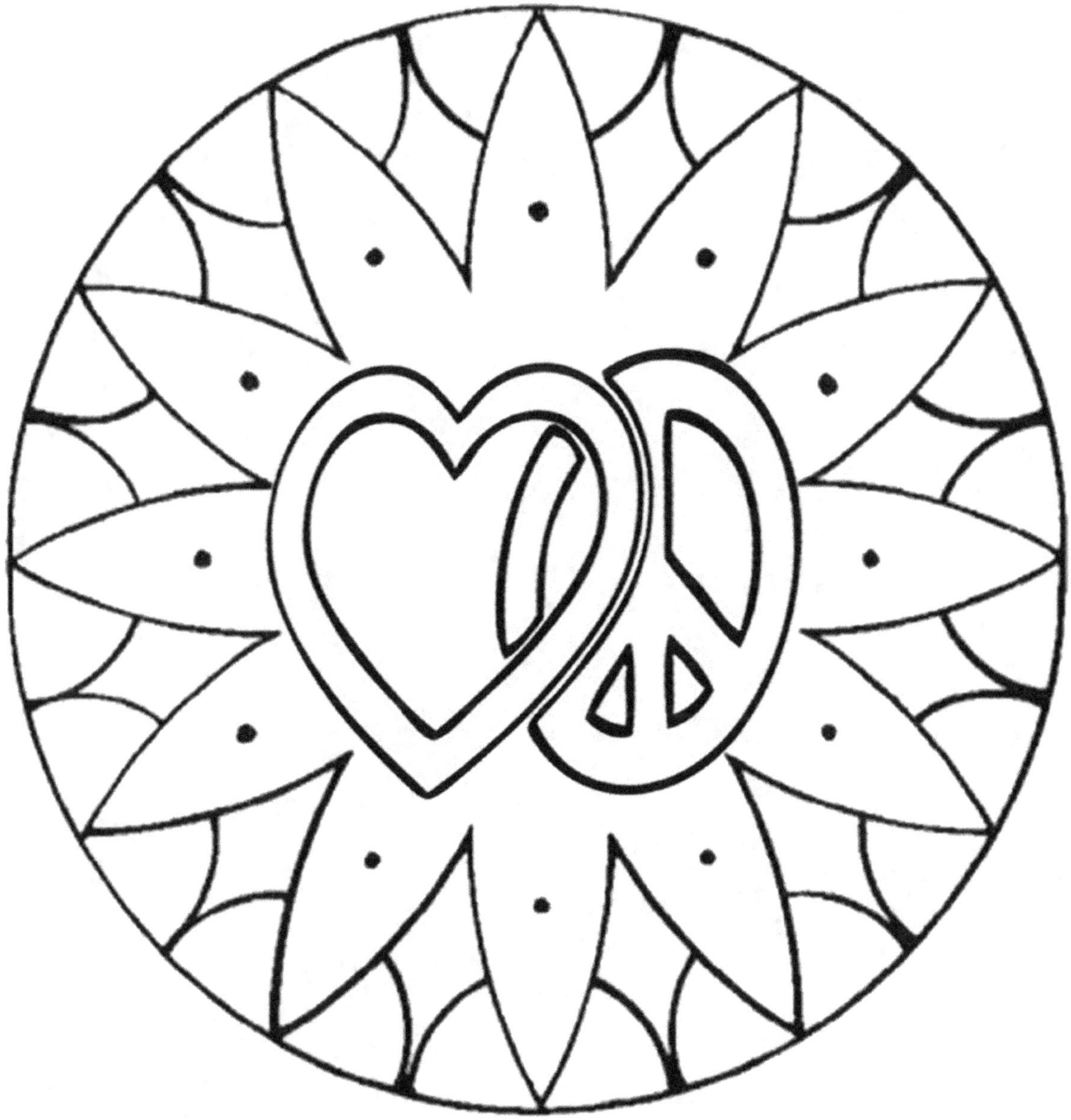

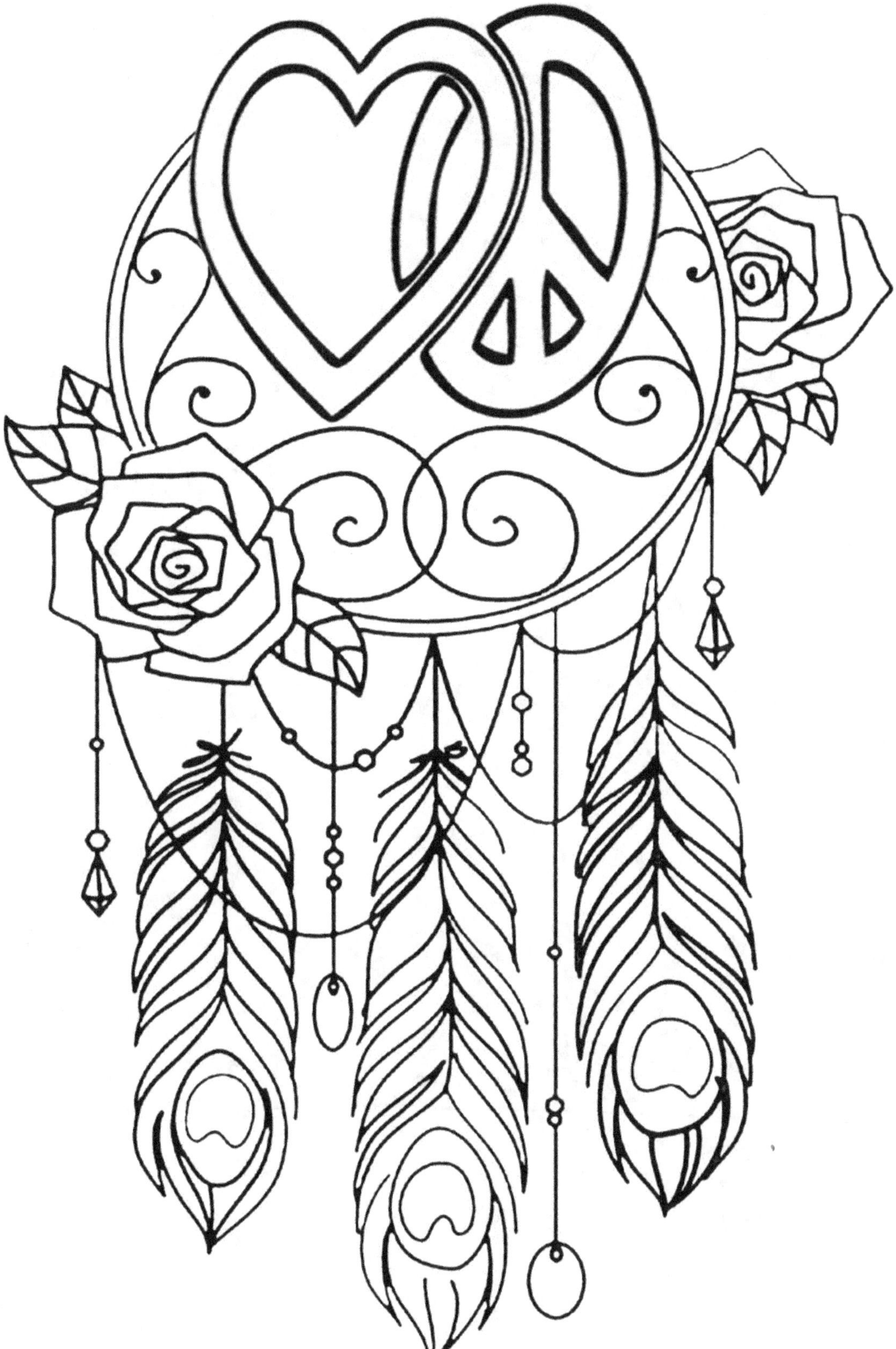

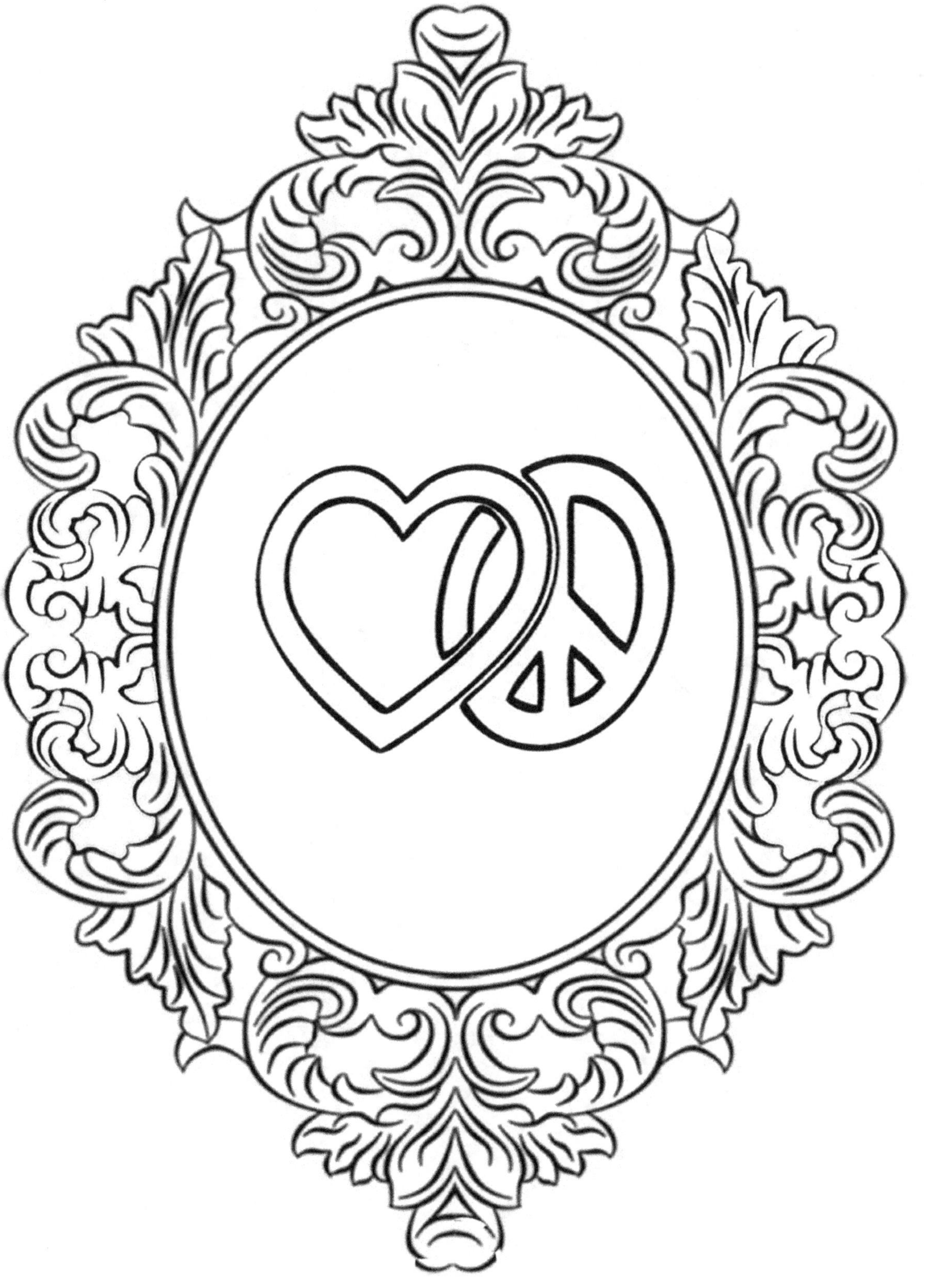

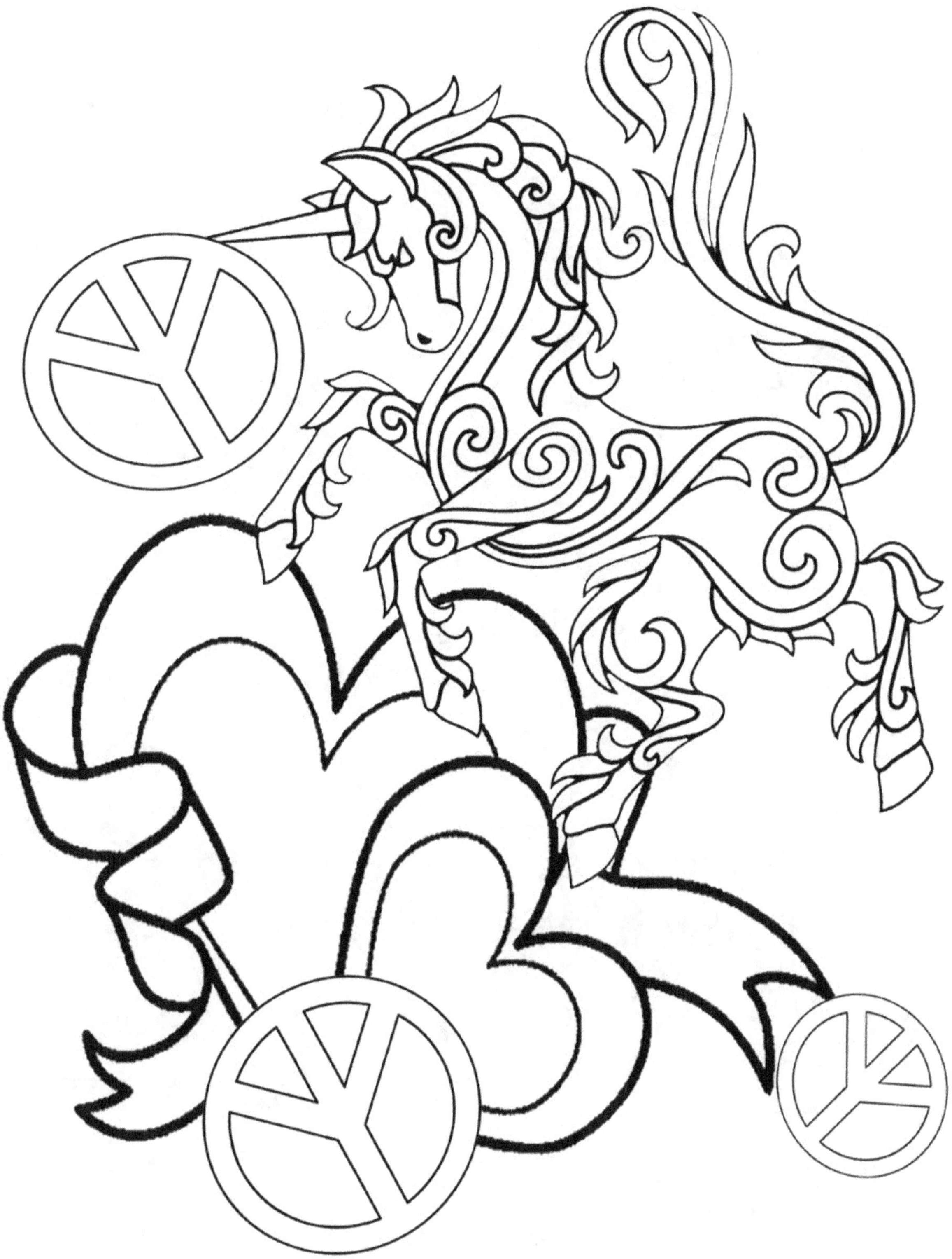

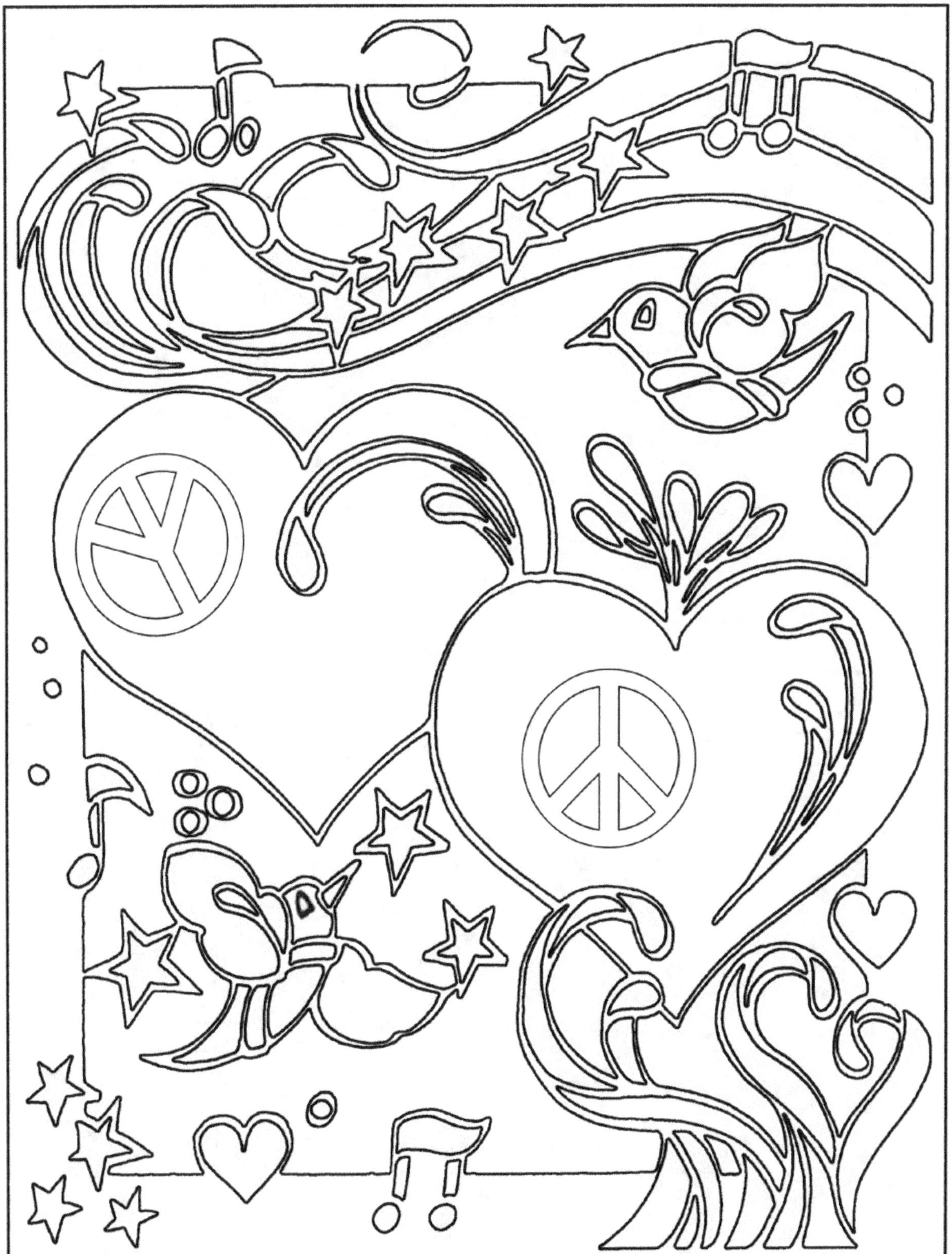

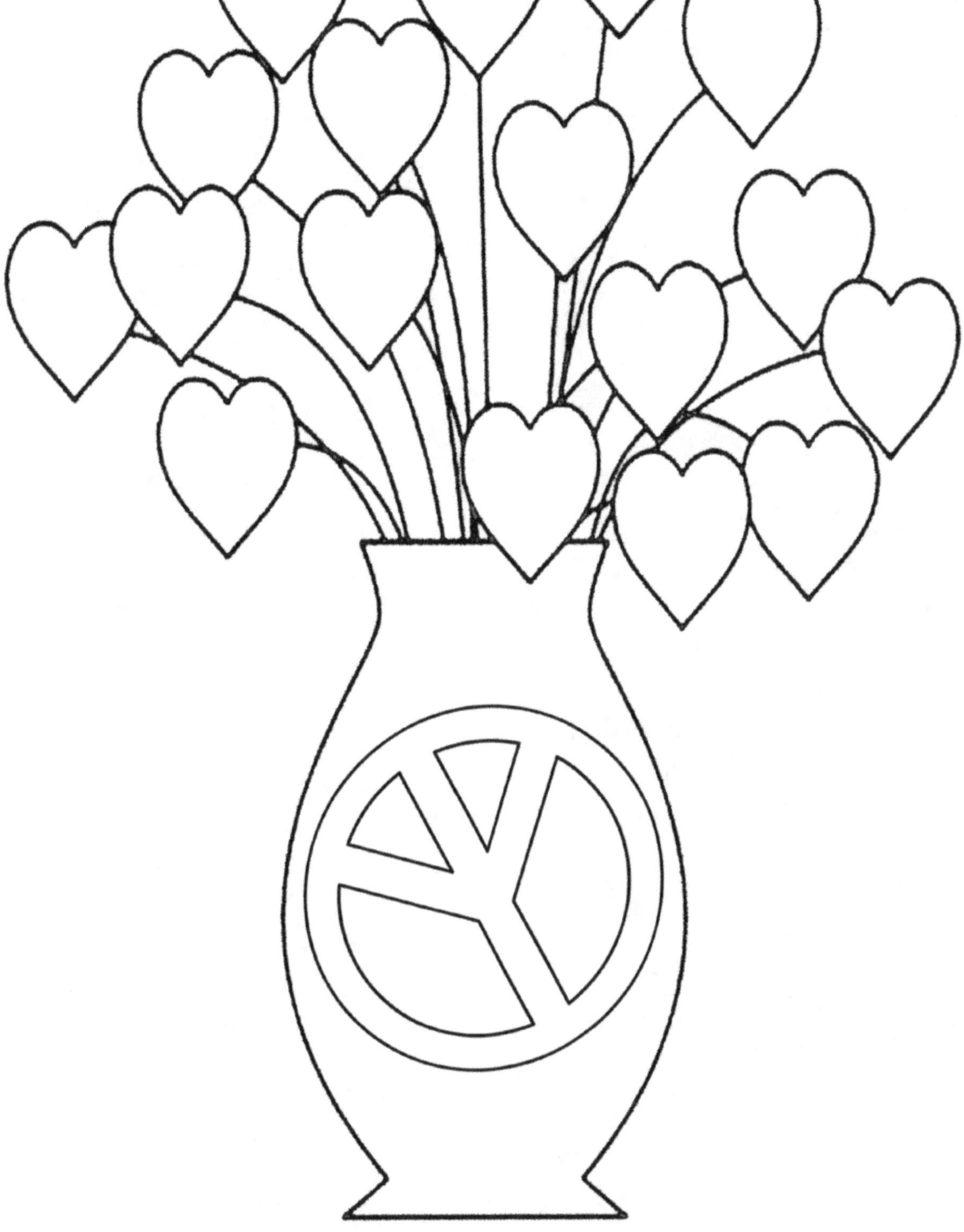

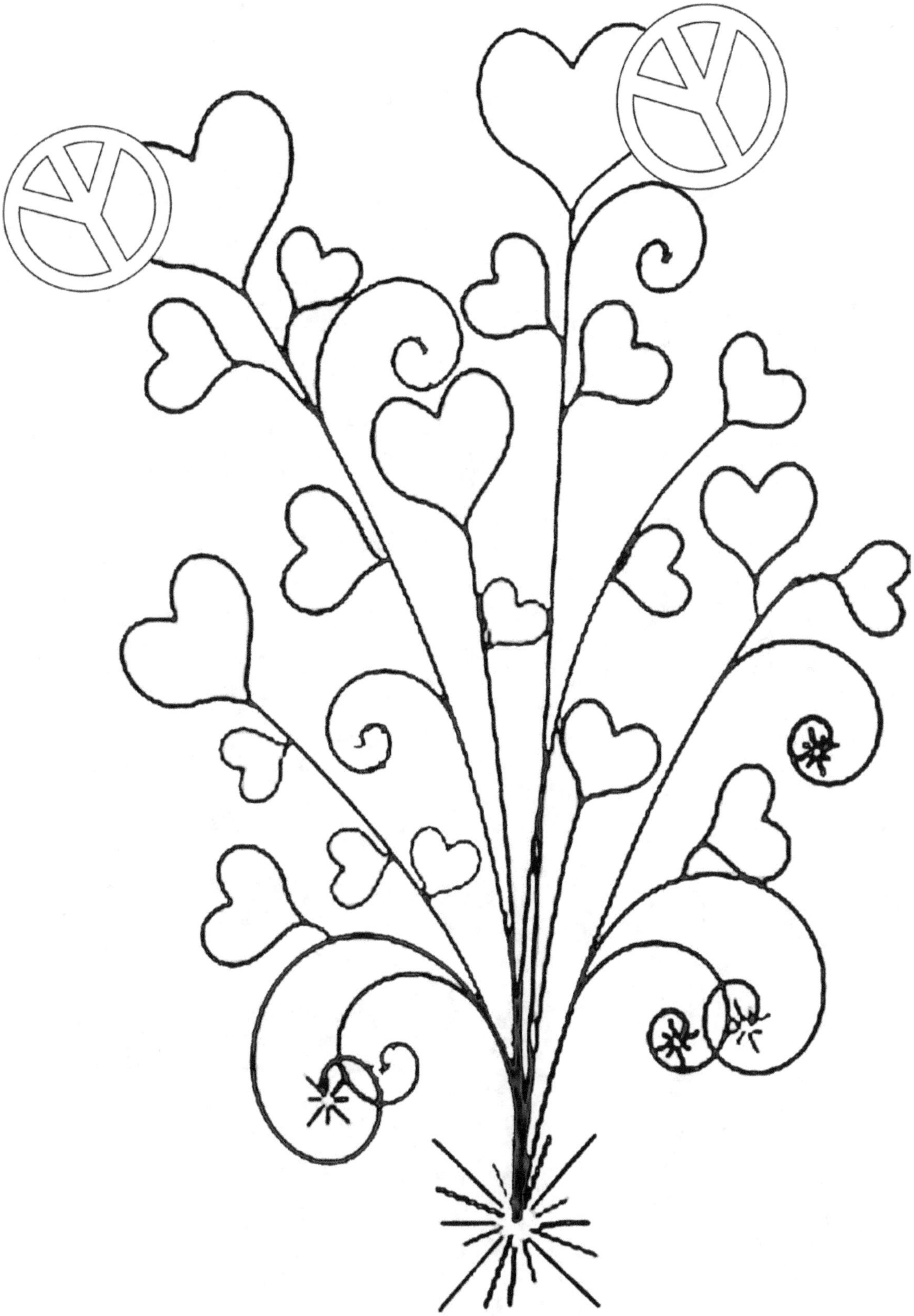

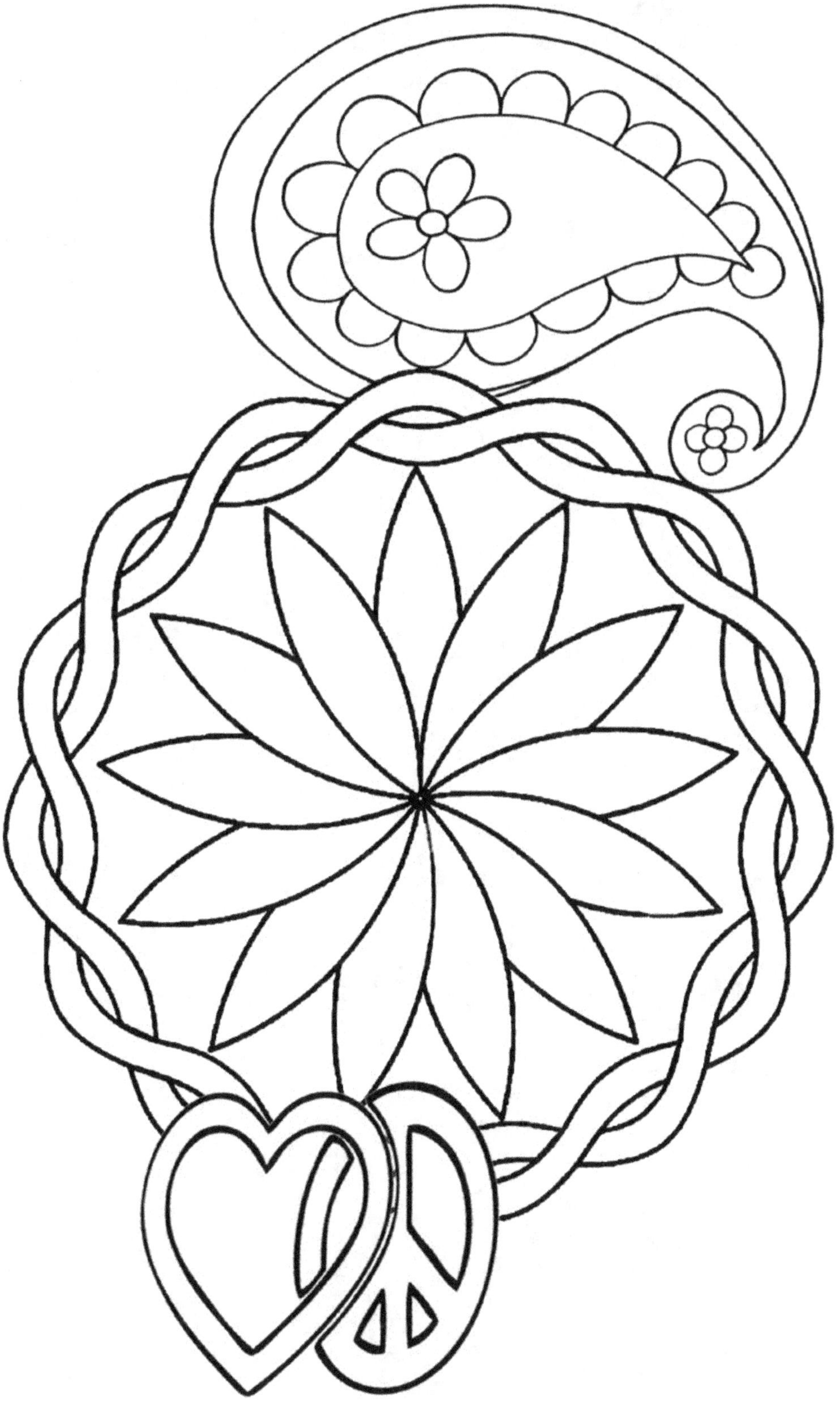

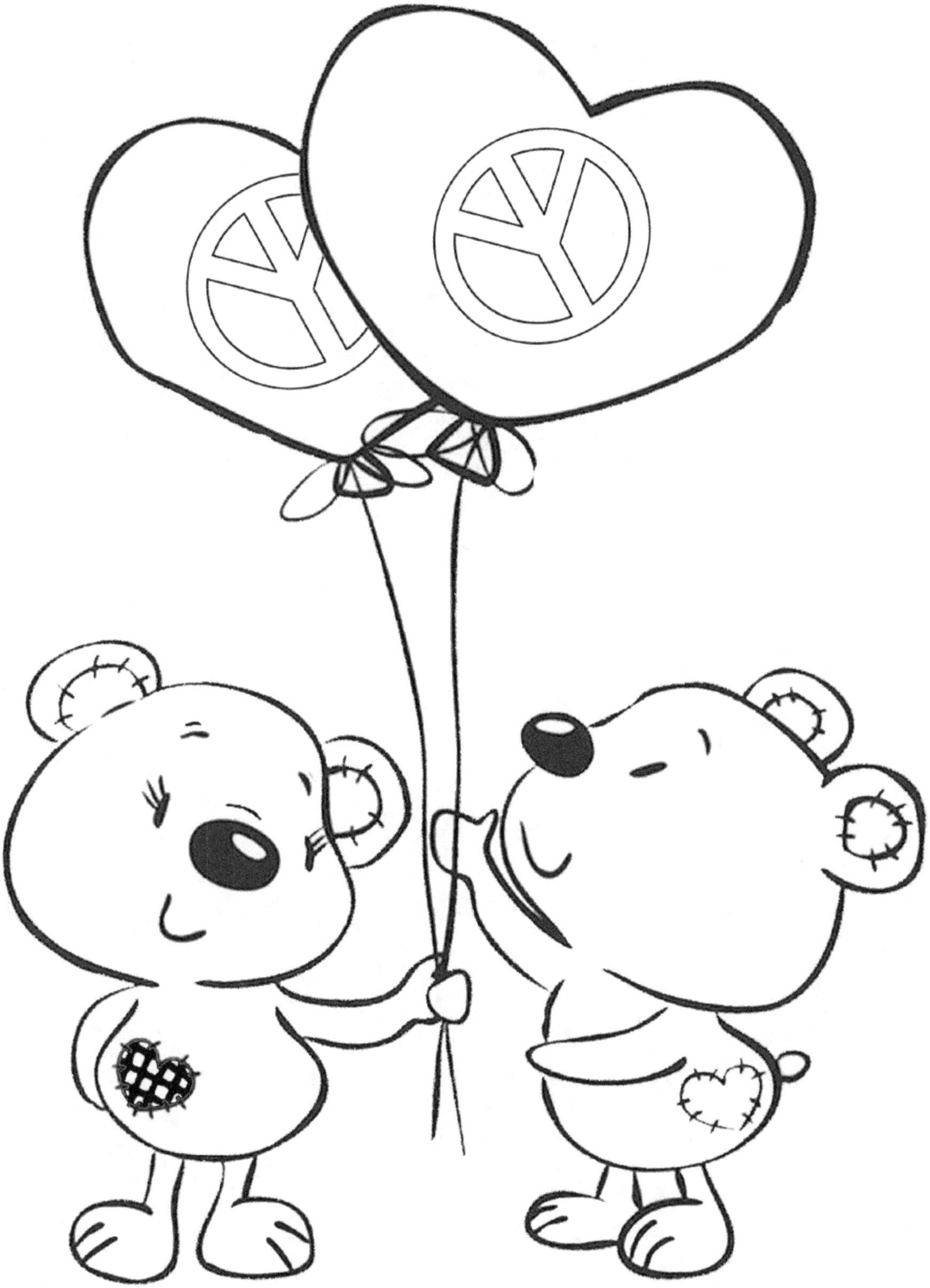

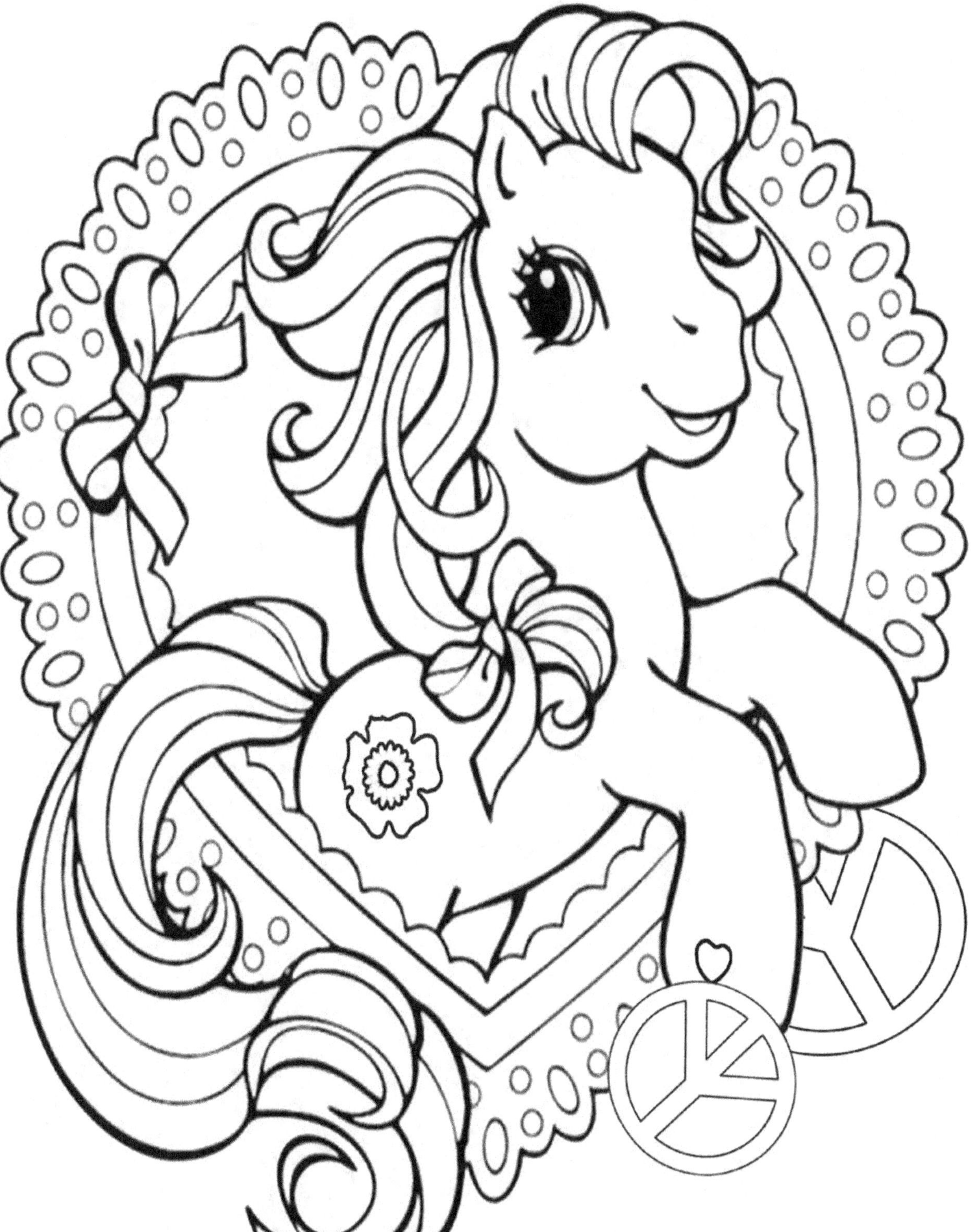

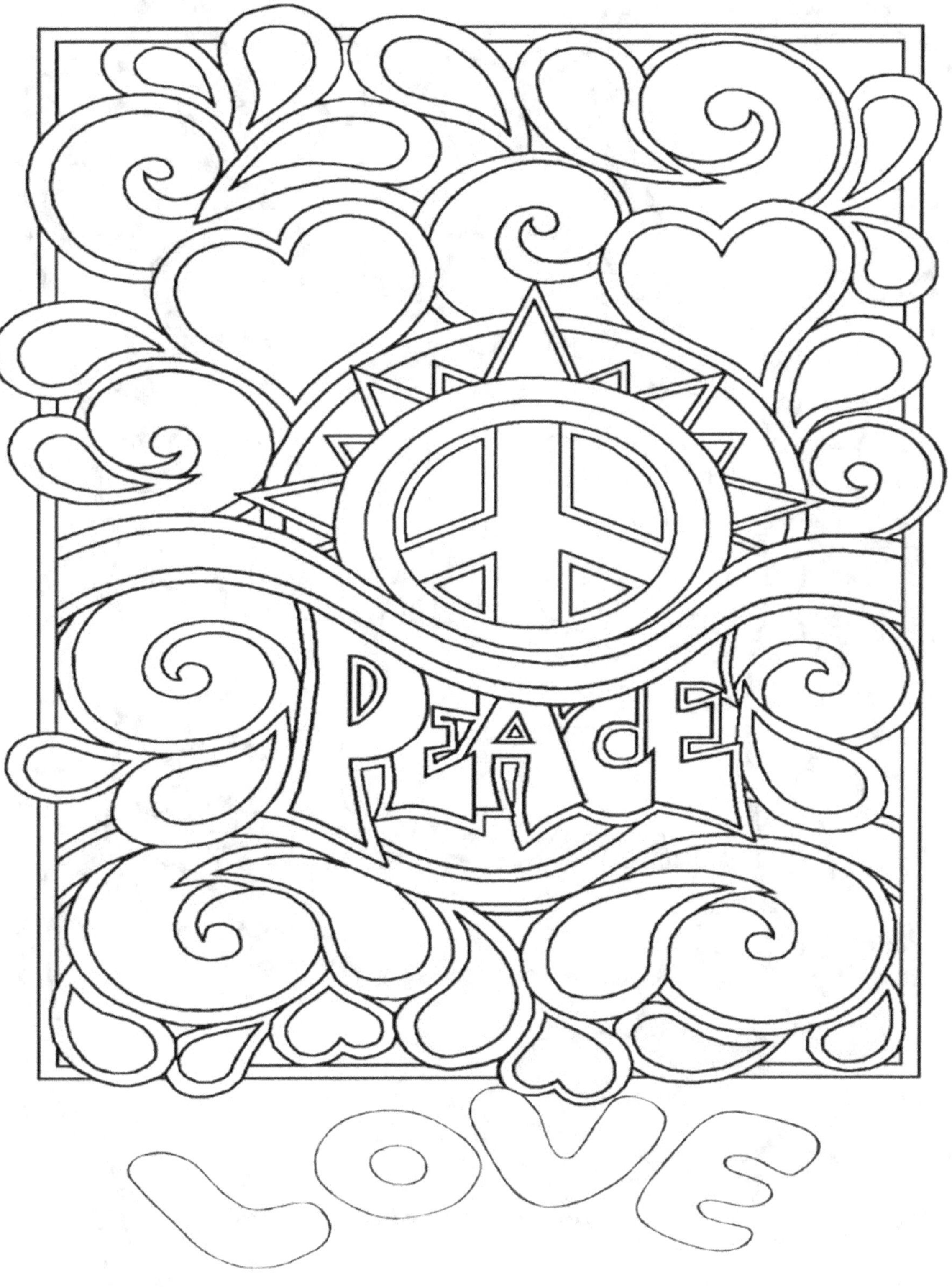
PEACE
LOVE

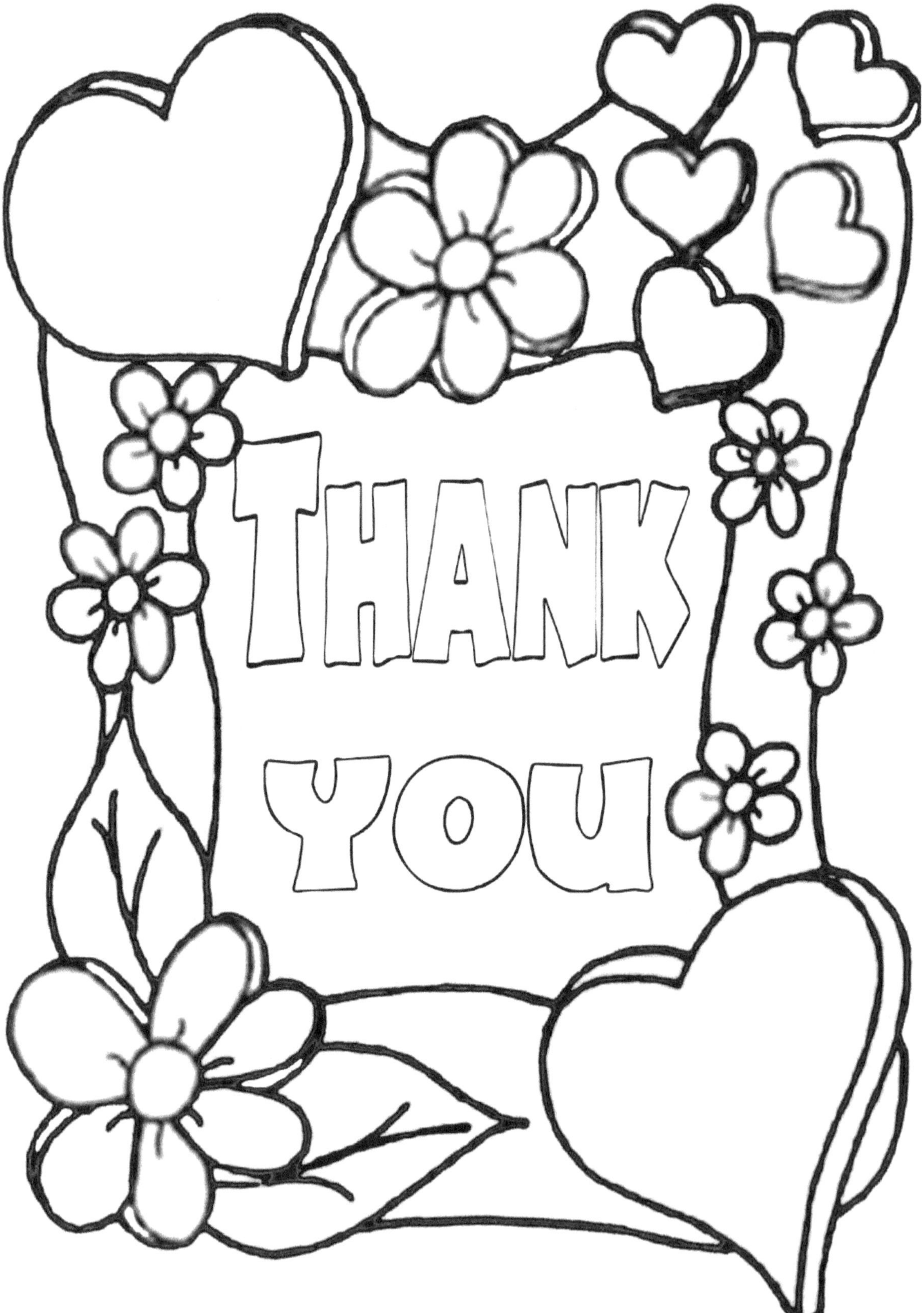
THANK
YOU

www.ingramcontent.com/pod-product-compliance
Lightning Source LLC
Chambersburg PA
CBHW081615220526
45468CB00010B/2881
* 9 7 8 1 9 8 3 9 2 9 8 9 2 *